Pipaluk and the Whales

John Himmelman

□ NATIONAL GEOGRAPHIC SOCIETY

Washington, D.C.

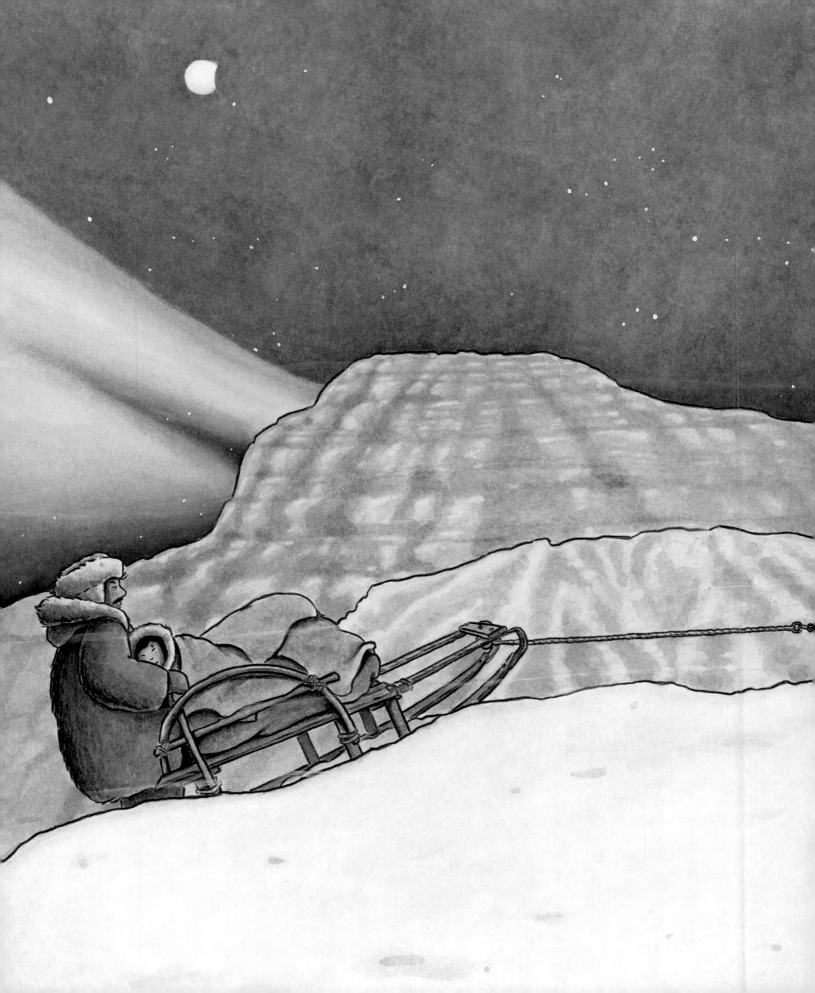

The night was bitter cold.
Pipaluk shivered, but she did not complain. She squeezed
closer to her father as their sled carried them home. This
had been her first hunting trip. The food and warm pelts
would help get them through the long winter.

"You will make a good hunter, Pipa," said her father.

Pipaluk smiled. Her father's warm words melted some
of the chill from her bones.

The dogs pulled the sled swiftly through the Arctic
night. Then suddenly, they stopped and began
to howl and cry.

"The dogs can hear what we cannot," said
her father. "Something is wrong. We will
let them lead us."

Pipaluk listened hard. All
she heard was the wind.

The dogs brought them to a ledge. Pipaluk and her father looked in the distance.

"The ice is moving!" shouted Pipaluk.

"That is not ice, Pipa, those are whales!"

They were beluga whales. She had often seen the whales gathering in the *savssats,* or ice holes, but never had she seen so many! So many beluga whales in one place would provide the village with enough food to last for many seasons.

Pipaluk and her father moved closer to the whales. "The sudden cold has closed up the savssat. The whales cannot hold their breath long enough to swim beneath the ice to open sea. They will starve to death. We cannot hunt them this way," said her father.

"Why can't we hunt them?" asked Pipaluk.
"The whales have helped keep our people alive
for many centuries. We owe them too much to
slaughter them while they are helpless. We must
get help from the village."

The villagers gathered tools to cut the ice. They loaded sleds with tents and food and followed Pipaluk and her father to the savssat.

"The hole is growing smaller," said Olan, one of the elders. "The whales will drown if we do not keep it open."

Pipaluk and the villagers chipped away at the edges of the ice to keep it from freezing over. The whales were packed so tightly, Pipaluk could have walked across them to the other side of the savssat.

Their mouths seemed to be turned in gentle smiles. But they did not look happy. The whales moaned and whistled. It was a dreadful thing to hear. Pipaluk knew the whales sensed the danger they were in.

Olan knew they would need more than picks and axes
to free the whales. He sent a man to get help from a
fishing village. They could send a ship called an icebreaker.
It would be able to make a channel to the savssat.

Day and night the people of the village chipped away
at the edge of the opening. Even Pipaluk's little brother
wanted to help. Her mother would not let him, though.
She was afraid he would fall into the water. Pipaluk
watched the older whales push the young calves to the
surface so they could breathe. My mother would do that
for me, she thought, and she worked harder.

Many miles away, the icebreaker began its journey.

Days passed. The people worked day and night to keep the hole open.

"The whales are growing weak," said Olan.

"They are starving," said a woman named Ivalu. She went back to the village and returned with some of the fish that were to feed her through the winter. Soon other villagers began to share their food with the whales.

One night, Pipaluk sat at the edge of the savssat and watched a young calf. She looked into its large, dark eyes and saw a reflection of the stars. She wanted the calf to see many more nights filled with stars. Pipaluk was filled with such sadness, she could not hold it inside her.

She began to sing. It was a song for the little whale with the stars in its eyes. Soon, others joined in the singing. The whales grew silent as they listened.

The moon came and went and returned again.
The whales were very weak. Pipaluk sang to the
whale with the stars in its eyes. She sang to all
the whales. It made her feel better.

One night, Pipaluk was awakened by a noise. She looked out of her tent and let out a cry of joy. It was the icebreaker! At last, it had arrived. The people stood and cheered as the icebreaker inched its way toward them.

Finally the ship broke through into the savssat.

"Go! You are free!" shouted Pipaluk. But the whales would not follow the ship out to sea. They were afraid of the huge, dark giant that made so much noise.

"GO!" shouted Pipaluk. "GO!" But the whales stayed. She wanted to jump into the water and push them. She was so angry. Angry, and frightened for the whales.

Pipaluk heard Olan speaking to the ship's captain.
"I am sorry," said the captain. "We are running
low on fuel. If we don't set off, we will be trapped,
too." The captain went back aboard the ship.
It slowly turned around to head toward the ocean.

They can't leave! thought Pipaluk.

The ship was the whales' last chance. Pipaluk heard the huge chunks of ice squealing and crunching beneath the ship's bow as it made its way out through the channel. Pipaluk covered her ears and sang out loud so she would not hear the noise.

Some of the whales came to her.

"Don't look at me!" shouted Pipaluk. "Go with the ship!"
Suddenly, she had an idea. She ran to catch up with the
icebreaker. A couple of the whales followed her.

The captain saw what was happening. "Bring her aboard," he shouted to his crew. "The whales are following her song!"

Pipaluk was helped onto the ship.

"Keep singing," said the captain. "You've given me an idea." He ran inside the cabin.

Pipaluk thought about the calf with the stars in its eyes. She had to save him. So she sang. Her voice was loud. But the whales could not hear her over the ship's engines.

Moments later, the captain returned. Music was blaring out of the ship's speakers. "Let's see if they like the sound of classical music, too."

Then the most amazing thing happened. The whales began to follow the ship. The villagers cheered as they ran along the savssat. Pipaluk's father set out with his dogsled. He would wait for his Pipa at the edge of the sea.

The sun rose and set as the icebreaker pushed through the shrinking channel. At last, it reached the open sea. The whales were free.

The crew helped Pipaluk down from the ship. She ran
to her father. They stood and watched the whales leap and
swim in the open water. Pipaluk picked up a handful of
powdery snow and threw it into the wind in celebration.

The whale with the stars in its eyes swam up to
her. Pipaluk knelt down and stroked its head.

"Stay out of holes in the ice," she whispered.

The whale gave a quiet whistle and then joined
its family in the sea.

"Come, Pipa. Let's go home," said her father.

Pipaluk climbed onto the sled. She shivered within the layers of fur she wore. But she did not complain. She squeezed closer to her father as their sled carried them home under the winter sky.

RUSSIA
(At the time of the story, Russia was part of the Soviet Union.)

CHUKCHI SEA

Siberia

Chukchi Peninsula

ARCTIC CIRCLE

Where the whales were trapped

Seward Peninsula

ALASKA
(United States)

BERING SEA

| 0 | miles | 200 |
| 0 | kilometers | 400 |

Newspaper photo of the February 1985 beluga whale rescue, copyright © ITAR-TASS Photo Agency

Author's Note

Pipaluk and the Whales is based on a true story that took place off Russia's Chukchi Peninsula. In December 1984 a Chukchi hunter discovered several thousand beluga whales trapped in an opening in the ice. He knew that if nothing were done to free the whales they would all die.

When the Soviet (Russian) government learned about the whales, it sent an icebreaker called the *Moskva*. The ship finally reached the whales at the end of February, after cutting a 12-mile-long channel through the ice. But the whales refused to follow the ship to the open sea. Scientists on the *Moskva* decided to see if they could lure the whales with music. They tried several kinds. It was classical music that finally led the whales to freedom.

For the Connecticut "Corps of Discovery"

Thanks go out to Steve Schuch, who in 1993 shared an article about this whale rescue.

Text and illustrations copyright © 2001 John Himmelman

The artwork is watercolor and colored pencil.

Text is set in Mrs Eaves Roman; display text is set in Allise.
Book design by Lyle Rosbotham

Library of Congress Cataloging-in-Publication Data
Himmelman, John.
Pipaluk and the whales / by John Himmelman.
p. cm.
Summary: Pipaluk and her father enlist the aid of their villagers and even the government
to help save a group of whales stranded in a frozen inlet, but only Pipa
can figure out a way to finally lead the whales back out to sea.
ISBN 0-7922-8217-5 (Hardcover)
[1. Whales—Fiction. 2. Chukchi—Fiction. 3. Arctic regions—Fiction.]
I. Title.
PZ7.H5686 Pi 2002
[E]—dc   2001000132

Printed in the United States of America

The world's largest nonprofit scientific and educational organization, the National Geographic Society was founded in 1888 "for the increase and diffusion of geographic knowledge." Since then it has supported scientific exploration and spread information to its more than eight million members worldwide. The National Geographic Society educates and inspires millions every day through magazines, books, television programs, videos, maps and atlases, research grants, the National Geographic Bee, teacher workshops, and innovative classroom materials. The Society is supported through membership dues, charitable gifts, and income from the sale of its educational products. Members receive NATIONAL GEOGRAPHIC magazine—the Society's official journal—discounts on Society products, and other benefits. For more information about the National Geographic Society, its educational programs and publications, and ways to support its work, please call 1-800-NGS-LINE (647-5463) or write to the following address:

National Geographic Society
1145 17th Street N.W.
Washington, D.C. 20036-4688
U.S.A.

Visit the Society's Web site: www.nationalgeographic.com